WALTHAM ABBEY

The Abbey of
Waltham Holy Cross and St Lawrence

A message from the Rector

For over a thousand years, the church at Waltham has been a place of Christian worship. During this time, innumerable people have prayed in this glorious 'House of God'. Kings, commoners, the famous and the humble, have entered this holy place and have found here the peace, the love and the inner strength which come only from Our Lord.

Whether you come from far or near, you are welcome, and we hope and pray that during your visit you will find, as may truly be said of the church, 'How awe-inspiring is this place! This is no other than the house of God, this is the gate of Heaven' (Genesis 28, v.17).

May God bless you and yours.

This lovely old church is primarily a very active parish church, but it is also a place of great historical importance. Founded by Harold, Earl of Wessex (later King of England) about the year 1060, it is a grand example of Norman architecture. Its history, however, begins even earlier – in about the year 1030.

BELOW: *The canopied west door, the entrance to the Abbey before the tower was built over it. It replaced a Norman door when the 13th-century west front was added. The carved stone head incorporated into the decoration above the door is of St Lawrence.*

RIGHT: *East windows and reredos.*

THE LEGEND OF THE HOLY CROSS

A carpenter, living in the village of Lutegaresburh (now Montacute) in Somerset, was told in a dream to get the villagers together and go to the hill above the village and dig there. At first he ignored the dream, but it returned nightly until he was compelled to do as he was bidden. In due course the villagers, singing a solemn litany, processed to the hilltop and there dug to a great depth where they found a marble slab cracked in two. Lifting this marble slab they uncovered a life-size black stone crucifix with the figure of Christ exquisitely carved. There were also a smaller crucifix, a bell and a book. The lord of the village was Tovi the Proud, a high official under King Canute. He owned many estates, one of which was here in Waltham. Loading these treasures (except for the smaller crucifix) on an ox-waggon, drawn by 12 red oxen and 12 white cows, he decided to take them to one of the great religious centres of England, or, failing that, to one of his estates; but the oxen refused to budge until Waltham was mentioned, at which word the cart shoved the oxen and came to this place. The coming of this Cross gave the name to the town which was called until recently Waltham Holy Cross.

It is difficult to disentangle fact from fiction in this fascinating story. Tovi the Proud was a real person, and Montacute, with its hill overlooking the village, is there for all to see. An intriguing possibility is that the objects found buried at Montacute had been taken there from Waltham, which we believe was a thriving community in the 7th century, in order to protect them from the desecrating Vikings in the 9th century. Other life-size crucifixes are known to have existed in the Anglo-Saxon period, and some, like the one found at Montacute, were credited with miraculous powers.

Waltham at this time was a clearing on the edge of the great forest of Waltham (now a much diminished Epping Forest), and, we are told, nothing was here except a hunting lodge belonging to Tovi. Sixty-six people joined the procession of the Holy Cross and founded the town. Tovi housed the Cross in the village church, installing two priests to minister to local needs.

THE HISTORY OF WALTHAM ABBEY

Athelstan, Tovi's son, succeeded to this estate on his father's death, but, since he proved a waster, it reverted to the Crown. Edward the Confessor gave it to his brother-in-law, Harold Godwinson, who built a large religious house, probably in the late 1050s.

The Cross of Waltham, bringing with it a reputation for healing, was believed to have cured Harold of paralysis and for centuries, during medieval times, Waltham was a centre of pilgrimage for people seeking its healing aid. Harold raised his minster here on the edge of the forest, to the glory of God and as a fitting house for the Cross.

There must have been quite a stir when masons, builders and carpenters descended on this lonely little community; when a small tributary of the river Lea disgorged bargeloads of stone from Caen, and a mighty edifice arose in their midst. Archaeological investigations have shown that the church built by Harold was of T-shape, with the nave walls re-using foundations from an earlier church. The continuous transept, the head of the T, would have been roofed straight across the roof-line of the nave.

1066 saw Harold's victory at the Battle of Stamford Bridge, but this was swiftly followed by the fateful news that the fleet of William the Norman had been sighted off the south coast.

Marching his tired troops down to meet the new enemy, Harold passed nearby and called in at his beloved minster. Here was the miraculous Cross that had granted him health. Would it grant him victory? As he prayed before it Turkill, the Sacristan, watched him. Turkill records that, as Harold prayed, the figure of Christ bowed to him and thereafter always looked down instead of upward as formerly. This was seen as an ill-omen but Harold went on to his tragic end. The war-cry of the Saxons as they bore down on the Normans was 'Holy Cross!'. Two priests from Waltham accompanied the Saxon army. After the disaster, they sent for Edith Swan-Neck, Harold's great love, who sorted through the carnage and found Harold and his brothers whom she brought back to Waltham. Harold is unlikely to have been buried behind the high altar, as this position was normally reserved for accredited saints; no reference is known to connect Harold with sainthood. The original burial was probably further west, in front of the altar of the

ABOVE: *The tower stairs. The ancient stone steps are so worn that oak treads have had to be fitted.*

LEFT: *Marks on a pillar caused by the swinging chains of books which once hung there.*

RIGHT: *The paintings on the nave ceiling represent the Four Elements, the Past and Future, the Signs of the Zodiac and the Labours of the Months.*

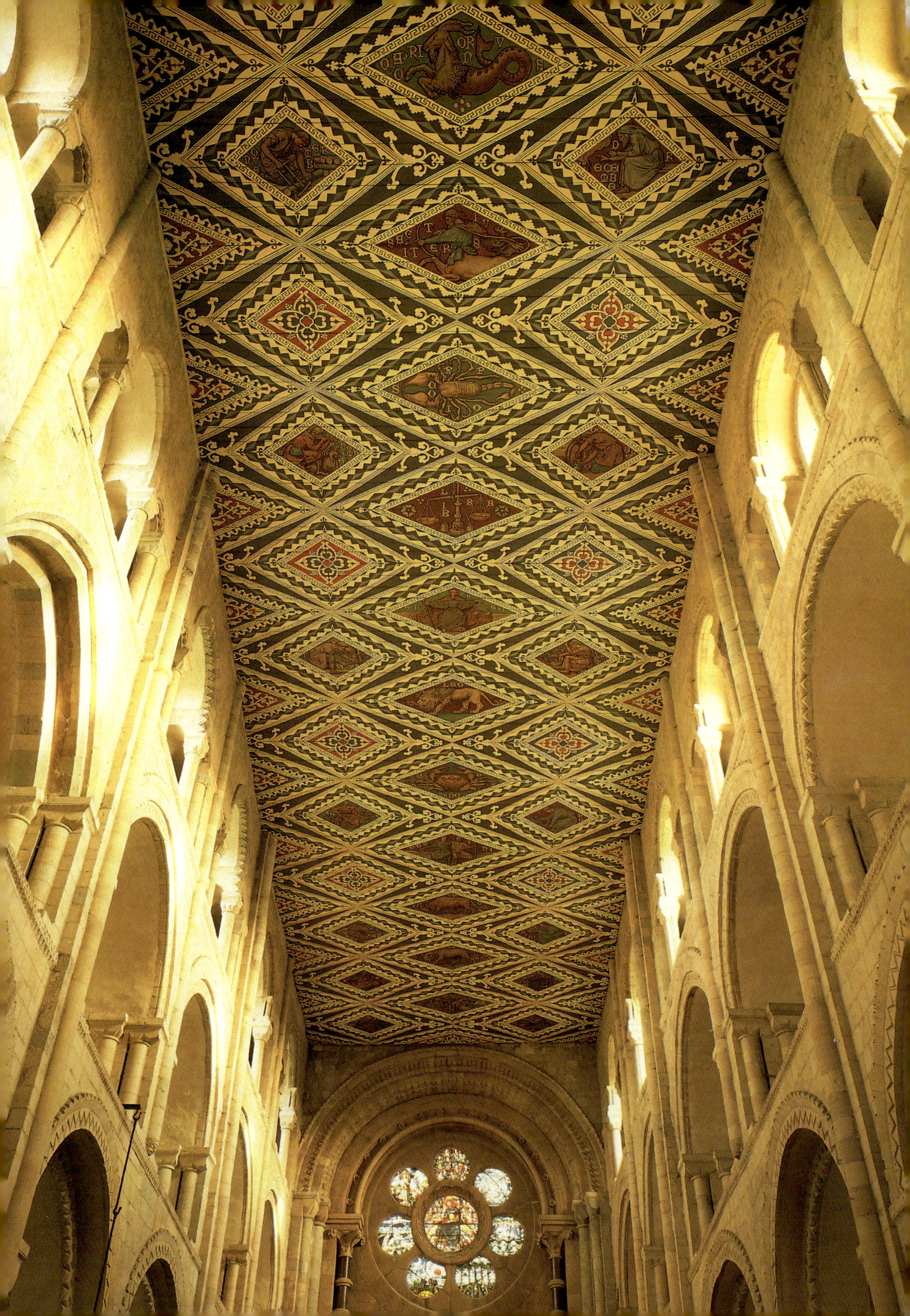

BELOW: *The ornately carved 17th-century tomb of Robert Smith, captain and owner of a merchantman, is in the north aisle.*

church he built. This would follow the example of Edward the Confessor, and was in turn followed by several subsequent kings down to Stephen (1135–54). Harold's remains were recorded to have been moved three times by 1200, and one late-12th century writer mentions 'king Harold lying in the choir'.

After the murder of Archbishop Thomas Becket in 1170, the king, Henry II (who was ultimately responsible for it), enlarged the church to three times its present length as one of the penances for his part in the murder.

In about 1060, Harold had arranged an elaborate series of rules for the discipline of 12 canons under a dean, but the individual nature of these rules rendered them difficult to enforce over a long period. In any case, a community of priests who did not fully practise communal life was an anachronism by (at the latest) the middle of the 12th century and the king, with the support of the pope, was able to replace Harold's college by the larger community governed by the rules of the Augustinian Order (1177).

From 1177, Henry's benefactions were so great, and the size of the church so large, that it is suggested he was intending to establish a family mausoleum in the church, probably in the middle section. If so, he must have changed his mind, since he cut off the money grants in 1184 before the work was complete; and having arranged for the pope to grant the title of abbot to the head of the house, Henry was eventually buried in France in 1189.

In 1286 repairs were needed and whoever was in charge considered the architecture of the Norman church to be out of keeping with the glories of Henry II's building with its tall pillars and high arches, and decided to alter the Norman fabric so that it conformed to the later style. His work can be seen in the two westernmost bays and the point at which he realised his error, the third triforium arch on the north side. Here the weakening of the building became apparent and he had to stop, but not before he had added a new and up-to-date west front. The evidence of the original Norman arches can still be seen in the stonework.

The dissolution of the monasteries began in a small way in the 1520s, but it was not until 1540 that Henry VIII came to Waltham Abbey – the last of the monasteries to be destroyed. He had a soft spot for Waltham; he was here often and had plans to make a cathedral of it. These did not materialise and its destruction was authorised in 1544. The townsfolk protested that the monastery lay to the east of their church and so the present building, with a tower at the east end, was saved for parish use. The splendour of Henry II's building was reduced to rubble.

In 1552, having been deprived of its supporting walls, the tower then standing at the east end collapsed. This injury to the fabric appears to have had little effect on the rest of the church. However, in 1556 many of the stones were transferred to the west end of the church and used in building a tower there to serve as a buttress and prevent the church from falling into Highbridge Street.

VICTORIAN RESTORATION

Your first impression of the interior of this grand church is the strength and simplicity of the Norman construction. The great pier arches support the smaller arches of the triforium with, above, the lesser arches of the clerestory. Then you notice the complete contrast with the ornate Victorian east end and ceiling.

This 1859–60 restoration was the work of the architect William Burges, whose friend Thomas Nicholls did the carving – but look at those windows, some of the finest Victorian stained glass to be found anywhere. Powells of Whitefriars made them from the cartoons of Burne-Jones who got £30 for designing the Rose window (Creation) and £20 for the Jesse window. Edward J. Poynter, who later became Sir Edward, president of the Royal Academy, executed the painted panels on the ceiling. These were designed by Burges and based on the ceiling in Peterborough Cathedral.

Visitors who imagine something occult behind the Signs of the Zodiac are disappointed to hear that these are no more than a representation of the months of the year, as seen by the ancients in the night sky. Bordering the ceiling are the Months with their appropriate Labours and, at the east end, Past and Future (an old man with an open book and a young woman with a closed book). Surrounding these are the four elements – Earth, Fire, Air and Water.

A large part of the cost of the restoration was paid for by the family of the Reverend James Francis, the incumbent.

ABOVE: *The Denny Tomb, 1600. Edward Denny, a champion of Queen Elizabeth I, was knighted for his services in Ireland and richly rewarded. Beneath the effigies of the knight and his wife, their ten children kneel in prayer.*

– 7 –

LEFT: *The entrance to the Lady Chapel. The screen was erected in 1886 in memory of the Reverend James Francis, vicar 1846–85, under whose guidance the interior of the Abbey was restored.*

RIGHT: *The high altar seen through a Norman arch. The reredos, by Thomas Nicholls, contains four panels depicting the Annunciation, the Angel and the Shepherds, the Visit of the Magi and the Flight into Egypt. The string course above illustrates two of Aesop's Fables.*

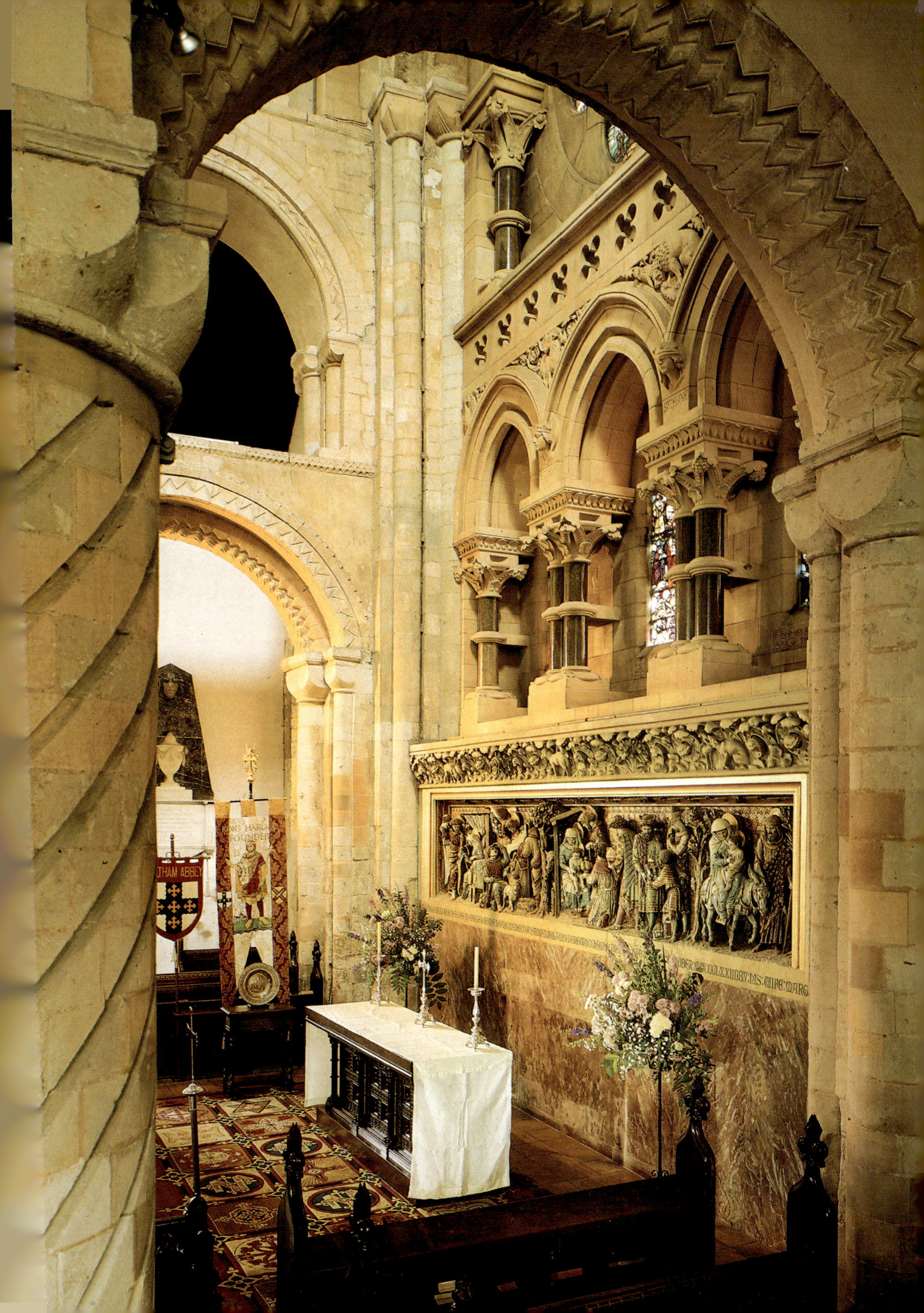
LTHAM ABBEY

ABOVE: *The 14th-century Lady Chapel, showing the 15th-century Doom Painting discovered in 1876 under the plaster and recently restored.*

A GUIDED TOUR OF THE ABBEY

Morning is the ideal time to view the east windows, when the sun reproduces the colours on wall and floor, but any time while there is light outside they are a joy to behold. From the altar rail the coloured carving of the reredos can be admired. It is a little later than the restoration, in memory of Samuel Bolton Edenborough who died in 1873. The beautifully carved walnut-wood altar was a gift from his wife.

Turn around and look at the organ casing at the other end of the church. Here is the coat of arms of Elizabeth I. It is worth remembering that Waltham Abbey (the town) was one place where the seed was sown from which the Reformation sprang.

In 1529 Thomas Cranmer (who was later to become Archbishop of Canterbury) came to Waltham as tutor to the sons of Robert Cressey, a local lawyer. King Henry VIII and his court were also here at the time. Cranmer, in conversation with the king's secretary, suggested that the question of the validity of the king's marriage to Catherine of Aragon (which Henry wished to have annulled) should be put to the universities of Europe, rather than only to the pope.

The left-hand one of the three tombstones beneath your feet has the date oddly written. At this time the 'Legal' New Year began on Lady Day (25 March) and until things were regularised in 1752 dates between 1 January and 24 March were recorded as shown on this tomb. Nearby is the slab dedicated to Thomas Leverton, the

WALTHAM ABBEY

BELOW: *A very active parish church. The congregation at parish communion, with the Easter Banners decorating the church.*

architect, and there is also a monument to him on the wall to your right.

Below is the remarkable tomb of Robert Smith (1637–97). This man captained his own merchant vessel and sailed the world to make his fortune. Here in great detail is depicted a vessel fighting wind and wave to avoid a rock. It is an allegorical picture of the Ship of Industry dodging the Rock of Sloth. The sea is full of fish and the bordering pattern of navigational equipment and funeral wreath and ribbons is meticulously carved in high relief. Note the hollow in the base of the sounding lead (bottom left) to take the tallow which picked up evidence of the sea bed and the knots where the string is tied under the top of the sand-glass (bottom right). The sculptor may have been Grinling Gibbons but there is no definite information on this.

The Purbeck marble slabs in the floor near this tomb are a 13th-century coffin lid and tombstone. The latter held the brass of an abbot of about 1300.

Looking across the church from this point, notice how the third arch from the left has buckled, how the shaft running up to the ceiling has bowed and how the triforium floor has sunk. It was found in a 19th-century restoration of the pillar (you will notice the different stone) that it had been built on 23 centimetres (9 inches) of clay. This clay was squeezed into a grave dug at this point soon after, and the building sank 23 centimetres at this point.

The block of wood up in the second triforium arch is evidence of the Rood Loft. An account for 1554, the first year of Queen Mary's reign, reads 'A John and Mary to stand in the Rood Loft – £2.6.8.' (John and Mary attended the crucified Christ). In 1558, the first year of Queen Elizabeth's reign, there is an account 'For taking down the Rood Loft – 3s.2d.'

ABOVE: *The middle lancet of the Jesse window. Jesse himself is represented at the base. The window was designed by Edward Burne-Jones in 1861.*

RIGHT: *The lovely Jacobean pulpit, removed during the 1859–60 restoration, but restored to its original site in 1964.*

Let us cross over now but, before we go up the steps into the Lady Chapel, look at the restored Denny Tomb. It shows Sir Edward Denny and Lady Margaret and their ten children. There are not six boys and four girls as you might think, but seven boys and three girls. The couple with linked arms are twins, Mary and Charles, and it was the convention not to separate them on tombs.

The sculptors were Bartholomew Atye and Isaac James of St Martin in the Fields. The monument was made in 1600 and cost £64. Isaac James was one of the great London masters of portrait sculpture. Lady Margaret survived her husband by nearly 48 years and is buried at Bishops Stortford.

Sir Edward's father, Sir Anthony Denny, acquired extensive lands in Waltham, which had previously belonged to the Abbey. Sir Edward's mother and Sir Walter Raleigh's mother were sisters.

The rather battered lady adjacent to this tomb is Lady Elizabeth Greville. She married Sir Edward's elder brother, Henry. Her father and Lady Jane Grey's father were brothers. The pieces of sculpture in the wall above this effigy were inserted here in the 19th century, having been found below the church floor. These are now believed to be part of a tomb of about 1300, the figure sculptures being of very high quality.

As you turn to climb the steps into the Lady Chapel, look up at the top window at the further end of the aisle. You will make out three steps at its bottom right hand. This is not just a window but part of a passage enclosed in the thickness of the wall. There is no exit or entrance today, but inside the wall at the left-hand side of the door, up by the left-hand side of the window across which you see it, and up through the thickness of the wall goes a passage of stone steps.

No-one has used that passage for over 400 years, yet the steps are completely worn out. Thousands of people must have walked those stones to wear them to this extent and it is possible that at one time pilgrims went this way to see the Holy Cross of Waltham. Where is that Cross today? Could it have been hidden by local people when the Abbey was dissolved?

The lovely Lady Chapel is entered through a 19th-century screen erected in memory of the Reverend James Francis. You are now outside the Norman church, as can be seen from the windows to the right and to the left of the large arch, which has swallowed up a third window. The mid-14th century walls, which are virtually two great windows, are tucked under the arm of a transept. Note the double tracery in the west window taking the stresses imposed. This chapel was much desecrated in the past. The windows were bricked up, leaving a small light in the centre of each of the four south windows. The place was boarded off from

WALTHAM ABBEY

the church, the walls were plastered over and the carvings smashed. It was used as a schoolroom and as a store, and the crypt below as a prison and later as a burial vault. In the 19th century, Sir Thomas Fowell Buxton, a local worthy, spent a great deal of his personal fortune in restoring the chapel to its former glory.

During this restoration the 15th century 'Doom Painting' was revealed. Here we have Christ sitting in judgement while angels blow the Last Trump. The dead rise from their graves and are weighed in the scales. This way to the Heavenly mansions and that to the jaws of Hell breathing out fire and demons! Such paintings were once very common, but comparatively few have survived to the present day.

Notice the Old English sheepdog in the stained-glass window showing the Nativity scene. Its original must have been a pet of the person commemorated in the window.

Beneath this chapel is the crypt, now a visitor centre. On the window sills are pieces of stonework, notably the 14th-century 'Waltham Madonna' dug up in 1974 in a garden on the north side of Sun Street. The seated figure is headless, and the Christ Child lost – the damage done before the statue was buried.

ABOVE: *The Abbey from the south. On the extreme right of the picture is the reputed site of King Harold's grave.*

RIGHT: *The west front. The present tower was built in 1556 with stones from demolished buildings. It holds one of the finest peals of bells in the country.*

Nearby is the organ console with its reminder that Thomas Tallis was organist in this church at the time of the Dissolution. In the mid-19th century the then organist, Dr W.H. Cummings, set Charles Wesley's words of 'Hark the Herald Angels Sing' to Mendelssohn's tune, without which no carol service is complete. Look out for the pillar by the south door bearing the mark of the links which secured the chained books. On the wall nearby is the brass of Thomas Colte; Sir Thomas More's first wife was of his family.

Near the west door is the monument to the fallen of the 'Rough Riders' (Imperial Yeomanry) raised by Colonel Colvin of Monkhams Hall in this parish for service in the South African War (1899–1902). In the porch notice the huge benefaction boards and coat of arms of Charles II above the west door.

There are some delightful figures hidden amongst the foliage carved on the capitals of the pillars here. See if you can find, on the north side, an owl with a feathered tail on one of the capitals and a dog on the other. On the south is a bird which has brought a worm for its offspring in the nest.

EPILOGUE

Three thousand words are not enough to convey all that could be said about this lovely old House of Prayer. We hope you found it something more than just an historic monument and if your 'visit' was only the reading of this guide, we hope you may one day come here in person and find for yourself the peace and serenity that, after so many centuries of prayer and praise, radiates from its stones, bearing witness to Jesus Christ, who is our sure Foundation and our living Lord.